Queen Mariella
and the Crow's Message

by

Dr. James P. Menconi

Illustrated by
Paula Lutz

Copyright © 2022 by Dr. James P. Menconi

ISBN: 978-1-998784-55-4 (Paperback)

978-1-998784-56-1 (E-book)

All rights reserved. No part of this publication may be reproduced, distributed, or transmitted in any form or by any means, including photocopying, recording, or other electronic or mechanical methods, without the prior written permission of the publisher, except in the case brief quotations embodied in critical reviews and other noncommercial uses permitted by copyright law.

The views expressed in this book are solely those of the author and do not necessarily reflect the views of the publisher, and the publisher hereby disclaims any responsibility for them.

BookSide Press
877-741-8091
www.booksidepress.com
orders@booksidepress.com

Dedicated to

Tyler Clementi

and all the other victims of bullying because we have to teach children early about the problems bullying creates;

to:

Salvatore Giunta,

U.S. Armed Forces Medal of Honor honoree, awarded for his bravery and courage shown in the War in Afghanistan.

and also to:

Marie Ella Menconi, Lynnette Menconi, Marvin Menconi and Richard Cozza who helped with the editing.

Language Key

"Niños, niños, paran su luchando ahorita"

"Boys, boys, stop your fighting now."

"Ramiro es su hermano."

"Ramiro is your brother."

""¿De veras, Ramiro? De versa, Ramiro

Really Ramiro?

¿Se lastimaré?

"Will he get hurt?"

"Vamos a continuar."

"Let's continue."

"Fantastico, Diego. Su familia es importante "

"Da respcto a su familia siempre"

"Pero Abuelito…"

""¡Pero Abuelito,,"

"But, grandfather,"

"Vengan aqui y ayudame."

"Come here and help me."

"¿Abuelito, que pasaré a Bianco?"

"Grandfather, what will happen to Bianco?"

"Abuelito no diga historias malas."

"Grandfather doesn't tell bad stories."

"¡Abuelito, esta era un historia maravilloso!"

"Grandfather, that's a great story."

"Fantastic Diego. Your family is important."

"Give respect to your family always"

"But Grandfather…"

Queen Mariella and the Crow's Message

"Niños, niños, stop your fighting right now¡ Boys, boys, paran su luchando ahorita!"

"¡Pero, Abuelito, he started it!"

"¡No es importante, Diego. Ramiro es su hermano. He's your brother, and you mustn't fight with your brother! ¡Vengan aquí y ayudanme! Come over here and help me plant some of these beautiful flowers. Planting the flowers will make you think of happier times. Notice how when you plant the white impatiens next to the red geraniums that both flowers stand out and look more radiant. This is how you two should behave with each other. You should always try to make your brother more brilliant and joyful just as the flowers in the garden make each other better and more colorful."

"¡Pero Abuelito,, but Grandpa, Ramiro took my Buzz Lightyear away from me!"

"That's okay, you need to share with your little brother and show him how you can play together in harmony. And that reminds me of another story. Let me tell you a story about how two brothers learned how to get along with each other without hurting each other. These two brothers were the sons of Queen Mariella and Javier. You remember Queen Mariella and Javier don't you?"

"Oh yes, grandpa. I remember their pure and natural love for each other. And I remember how Javier fought to his death to get the magic potion from the peonies to save Queen Mariella."

"Good, Diego. That love is the same love you should have for your brother, Ramiro. You should always love and respect your brother for your family is very important. ¡Da respeto a su familia siempre! You will always cherish and carry this love and respect for your family in your heart wherever you go. This pure and natural love will also help you live harmoniously with your brother and others.

Sit and I will tell you this wondrous story. Now it came to be that the names of these two brothers born of the love between Javier and Queen Mariella were Dulio and Bianco. Dulio was a brave and strong drone ant like his father, Javier. He also was very popular with all the other drone and soldier ants. He enjoyed all sports such as wrestling, boxing, racing, soccer, and lifting heavy weights since he was a pure athlete like his father, Javier. His success in sports made him very popular with all the soldier ants and drones. The other ants always wanted Dulio on their team so that they had a better chance of winning. This also made him very popular with the lady ants since he was so athletic and successful in whatever he did. Whenever he played soccer, he always scored the winning goal. Whenever the soldier ants had to build an ant hill to show the other ants in the colony the way, Dulio was always the one who led the way. Dulio, however, loved to brag about his accomplishments and loved to play around and flirt with the lady ants. He always attracted a lot of attention.

Bianco on the other hand was very shy and reserved. Some say that he was just timid. He never socialized with the other ants. He spent much of his time by himself because he was afraid of what the others would say. He was always interested in nature; taking a nature walk or drawing pictures of the beautiful flowers. He liked reading and writing poetry. Some say that Bianco was different. He had different interests than Dulio. Instead of being with others, he preferred to read a book or paint by himself. Instead of working or playing with the others he preferred to be out and about discovering new things in Queen Mariella's magical garden."

"I think I'm a little different too, right grandpa!"

"¿De veras, Ramiro? Its okay Ramiro, it's good to be different. We're all different. The differences in people make the world a more vibrant place to live, just as the different colored flowers in my garden make it a more colorful and radiant garden; Therefore, we have to learn how to celebrate and accept these differences.

Dulio would often tease Bianco about him being shy and not wanting to have sport with his friends. He would say condescendingly to Bianco, 'What's up Bianco, you afraid to have sport with me and my friends? Or would you rather just waste your time playing with flowers and your silly animal friends?'

Sometimes, Dulio would even bully him into doing things he didn't want to do. One time, Dulio threatened Bianco by saying, 'You clean my room, or I'll make sure you never forget who's number one around here!' Then he punched him to make sure he understood. Bianco was very upset with this but he never told Queen Mariella. He kept it to himself causing him to lose sleep because he didn't think he was treated fairly by Dulio.

One day Dulio was out playing sport with his friends. Since they enjoyed wrestling the best, they decided to have some wrestling matches. They thought it was a good sport because it was fun to see who was the strongest of all the drone and soldier ants. Once the wrestling matches began, they would cheer each other on as they wrestled to see who was the strongest and the bravest. Dulio was always the first to volunteer for he enjoyed wrestling the most. His opponent for his first match was Sergio, who was an up and coming young soldier ant who loved all kinds of sport just like Dulio. Sergio really wanted to show everyone that he was the equal to Dulio, who always won the wrestling matches. Sergio wanted a name for himself, so he volunteered to fight Dulio.

After a long struggle with many twists and turns in the wrestling match, Dulio finally lifted his opponent in the air and threw him down hard, getting Sergio to tap out and lose. Everyone cheered Dulio's victory. Dulio, however, was very impressed with Sergio's courage and perseverance and decided that Sergio should fight again to show his merit.

The very next day, Dulio spoke to Bianco about coming to join his crew of friends who enjoyed sports. Dulio said to Bianco, 'Why don't you come and join us at the playground to see how much you'll enjoy being with us? Who knows maybe you'll even enjoy wrestling like we do instead of reading by yourself or going for nature walks?' With that being said, Bianco finally decided to join Dulio as he headed off to meet his friends. Bianco didn't want his brother to think that he was 'chicken' or that he didn't want to be friendly with his friends.

When Dulio and Bianco arrived at the playground, Dulio's friends all started shouting, 'Go for it Sergio, get Bianco. Show that little runt what courage is all about! Beat him good!' 'Go for it! Let's see some real wrestling action.' Even Dulio shouted, 'Let's go Bianco, wrestle Sergio and be a real drone!' knowing in his heart that Bianco would get a good beating since he had so little experience wrestling.

Little did Bianco know that he was to wrestle Sergio. Sergio was lean, muscular and strong from all his time wrestling and playing sports. Bianco was weak and frail because he spent most of his time reading, taking nature walks, or painting which he loved so much. Bianco, however, had no choice. He had to stand up for himself. He had to draw up all his courage within himself like Queen Mariella talked to him about when she told them about how courageous Javier, their father, was fighting the spiders to get the peonies' magic potion. Finally, he didn't want to embarrass himself in front of Dulio's friends, so he charged Sergio not knowing what to expect since he wasn't a fighter. When Sergio saw him charging recklessly he just pulled him to the side and threw him down with a great force as he laughed about Dulio's folly. Once he was down, he pounded on him and got him in a wrestling hold and pulled and pulled until Bianco screamed in agony. How humiliated Bianco felt. It seemed that the whole world was against him. When Bianco started screaming, all the other ants shouted 'Weakling, you're a loser and a coward. Go home to your mommy!'

When Sergio finally let him up, Bianco was more embarrassed than hurt from the sport so he just ran and ran as fast as he could not knowing; where he was going because he was so ashamed of himself. As he ran, he thought abou*t* what all the others would say. *He* kept on hearing the hurtful and tormenting words in his mind: 'Weakling, you're a loser and a coward.' Because of this he was embarrassed and didn't know what to do. He just kept running. His thought was to make the problem disappear. As he got farther and farther away, he ran through Queen Mariella's garden until he got to the Never-Ending Forest. Deep in his memory, he knew that at the end of the Never-Ending Forest he would reach the field of peonies where his father, Javier, fought so bravely to gather the peonies' wax to save Queen Mariella when she was sick. However, because he wasn't thinking, he forgot Queen Mariella's warning not to ever go into the Never Ending Forest unless he was accompanied with many soldier ants and drones.

Finally, he became so totally exhausted from his reckless running and running that he fell asleep right where he was, deep in the Never-Ending Forest. He was so totally exhausted that he didn't know where he was. As the night passed, all the creatures of the night like the raccoon, the owl, and the possums prowled around and saw that Bianco was all alone in the Never Ending Forest. Since the animals were friends of Bianco, they sent a messenger to Queen Mariella to tell her that Bianco was all alone and lost in the Never-Ending Forest."

"¿Abuelito, que pasaré a Bianco? ¿Se lastimaré? Grandfather what will happen to Bianco? Will he get hurt?"

"No, no, Ramiro!", said Diego. " Abuelito no diga historias malas. Grandpa doesn't tell bad stories. Ramiro."

"Vamos a continuar niños. Let's continue boys. ….

When Queen Mariella heard the message that Bianco was lost, she knew that Bianco had to be rescued. She feared that the bears or wasps would ravage him in an instant, for the wasps and bears are enemies of ants and their colonies. She became frantic, not knowing what to do first. She thought to herself about why Bianco would just run away without reason. Then she realized that his brother would probably know why he fled the colony so suddenly. She quickly called for Dulio to investigate the reason why Bianco would be so deep in the Never Ending Forest by himself.

When Queen Mariella confronted Dulio about why Bianco was reported lost and alone in the forest, Dulio had a blank stare on his face. He knew that Bianco fled the colony because he was embarrassed by Sergio and his other friends at the wrestling match, but he was afraid to tell her the truth. So at first, Dulio just stuttered saying nary a word. As his conscience bothered him, he blurted out, 'Bianco ran away because he lost the wrestling match with Sergio when we were having sport! He was embarrassed to lose! How could he face himself, son of Javier, losing a wrestling match with a lesser ant?'

'But why were you having sport in such a rough way? You know that Bianco doesn't take to rough sports well. That's not his nature. What is sport to you is death to him!' Queen Mariella replied.

'But he wanted to have sport with my friends. He wanted to show me that he was my equal.' Dulio answered, knowing that it wasn't entirely true.

'Well, you're going to have to take your soldier friends and follow his scent trail to find out where he is the Never-Ending Forest and rescue him. Just maybe when you find him, you can find enough mercy and understanding to treat him with more respect. For he is your brother and you need to accept him just the way he is. Hurry, for in the Never-Ending Forest, there are many dangers and ant enemies such as the wasps, widow spiders, and bears. To reward whoever brings Bianco back unharmed, I will provide him with an endless supply of honeydew (a source of sweet energy from aphids).'

Dulio knew that he then had to find his brother. However, he was mainly interested in winning the honeydew rather than saving his brother and his dignity. So Dulio gathered his soldier ant friends including Sergio to follow Bianco's scent trail and rescue him despite his fear of the widow spiders, wasps and bears in the Never-Ending Forest."

"Abuelito, is Dulio going to rescue Bianco?"

"We'll see Ramiro. Let's listen!! .....

As the sun rose above the Never-Ending Forest at the break of dawn, Bianco woke to a strange sound. It was the cawing of a crow. 'Caw-caw-caaaaw! Caw, caaaw!'

Recalling stories *in* ancient Native American Folklore, that Bianco remembered, the crow carried the spirit of dearly departed souls since they were the guardian and keeper of the law. So he listened carefully to the sound of the crow. He knew too that the crow is a sign that it may be time to examine your life and change it so you are morally and spiritually correct. The crow's voice will often ask you if you are on the right path. Or is it time for you to become better than you know yourself to be; a time to walk the walk, not just talk the talk.

As he listened intently to the crow, he heard his father's voice. 'Be courageous, my son. Stand up for your beliefs and your dignity. Realize who you are, be strong and never change for you are amazing just the way you are - - - - - - Never feel that you are less of an ant or living thing because of what you like or don't like - - - - - Never be bullied to be someone you are not. It is the others who must learn to accept you as you are. Have faith in yourself and stand strong to earn that pure and natural love Queen Mariella and I had Follow this path and you will be victorious.'

Once he heard that message, his heart was filled with joy, strength, and passion to be what he knew he could be; true to himself, Instead of seeking to be someone he wasn't' just to satisfy others. Now he knew that he needed to go back to Queen Mariella's colony and show everyone how he too could be a valuable part of Queen Mariella's pure and natural kingdom. Instead of running away and ending his life, He knew that now was the time to stand up for his rights and show everyone how important he is to others.

How important it is to enjoy nature, write, study, and being different. Just maybe one day his role in life would be important to others. Someday others would see that the message he learned here was that it wasn't important that he lost his wrestling match with Sergio, but that he became stronger because of it.

As he lifted his head to the sky above to watch the crow fly away, there appeared a field of peonies creating a bright, shiny, fluffy kingdom; a kingdom of hope and happiness. It was a kingdom where everyone was equal and no one was ridiculed or mocked. Bianco knew that here was the field of peonies where Javier and his soldier ants gathered the peony potion that was used to save Queen Mariella. Now he knew he was on the right path. This vision filled his heart with a pure and natural love. And now he knew he could return home to Queen Mariella's colony with respect and dignity.

As he turned in the opposite direction, back through the Never-Ending Forest to return home, he saw Dulio and Sergio leading their troop of soldier ants. When they came in vision, Bianco heard Sergio shouting, 'There's that fool! Let's get him!'

The sight of his brother and Sergio didn't stop Bianco; nor did Sergio's threatening tone. The crow's message had breathed new life into his soul. Instead he headed straight toward them filled with his father's courage. He no longer was going to be bullied. For now he knew that he had nothing to be ashamed of since his life was heading in the right direction. As he looked up to remind himself of the crow's message and his father, Bianco saw a cloud of wasps swooping down upon the troop of soldier ants in hopes of having a big meal. Bianco shouted out a warning: 'Take cover, the wasps are attacking, which placed him in great danger because he was in an open space.

The wasps flew down like lightning from the sky and clutched the soldier ants one by one till they were dead as door nails, ready for lunch. After only a few minutes all that remained were Dulio and Sergio since they were up front and the only ones in range of

Bianco's warning. Once they heard Bianco's warning they escaped by hiding under a rock. Bianco's warning had saved them.

After the wasps left with their meal, Bianco raced over to greet his brother and Sergio. Sergio apologized and thanked Bianco for the warning.. 'Thank you for saving our lives. Your warning spared us from the attack our friends suffered!' Dulio replied, 'No big deal. We're sport buddies and buddies stand up for each other when in need. .... We better get straight back to the colony. We have no time for sharing our feelings now.'

"Grandpa, that's was exciting!", exclaimed Ramiro. "I really liked how Bianco now became a hero in the eyes of his enemies, Sergio and Dulio!"

"That's right, Ramiro!" Grandpa said as he comforted Ramiro. "We all have a purpose. At times when you least expect it, you can see how important you are to others!

Now let's get back to the story......

As they traveled through the Never-Ending Forest, Sergio saw Bianco in a different light. He realized how courageous and fair Bianco was. Bianco could have said nothing to keep himself safe from the wasps and then they would have all perished. Instead he did his best to warn everyone of the approaching danger. As a result, he realized that Bianco was one of them; a friend, their equal.

As night approached, their travels became more difficult. Their scent trails leading back to the colony had weakened. The dangers in the forest became more frightening. There was always the threat of more wasps, lion ants, widow spiders, or bears. At times, they thought they were lost because the scent trail had weakened. So Bianco stood up straight and tall and gave them hope by telling the others that he had remembered a fallen, twisted twig as a marker for the true direction. When he did this, he realized that his love of nature had meaning. If he hadn't been interested in observing nature he wouldn't have had this keen sense of knowing where he was. As he reflected on what his father said in the crow's message, he realized that our interests in life have a purpose: It doesn't make you less of a living thing because of what you like or don't like.

Soon, Bianco knew they would arrive safely at home. Just as this thought came to mind, the edge of the Never-Ending Forest came in sight. Realizing this he shouted, 'Look the edge of the forest!' And just when he shouted out, alarming them all, a bear cub appeared rooting around for food. The bear cub swiped his paw in hopes of gathering lots of ants, but all that he grasped was one ant, Sergio. Dulio and Bianco escaped his grasp and headed for cover under a branch. In disgust, the bear cub flicked Sergio away. His sharp claws, however, tore him apart and Sergio died. As the bear departed, Dulio ran in fright not even thinking of anyone else. Bianco, instead, went to recover Sergio's body and carried his body all the way back to the colony for Sergio had lead a brave life and Bianco wanted to honor his new friend.

Bianco carried Sergio's body through Queen Mariella's garden without any help from his brother. He knew Queen Mariella would honor Sergio's bravery and memory. Now he had a greater purpose in life and all his self doubts and memories of the name calling left his mind. His greater triumph would be ahead when he and Dulio would see Queen Mariella once again.

Dawn finally arrived brightening their horizon, and Bianco knew there was hope for a safe arrival home. Their colony appeared as a shiny kingdom on a hill. When the other ants saw Dulio and Bianco arrive, their cheers of glee and relief filled the colony with hope and harmony once again. Queen Mariella knew her prayers were answered. Yes, there was a heavy toll because the only ones to survive the journey were Dulio and Bianco, but it was uplifting to see her sons once again.

Queen Mariella realized that it was time to pay tribute to those who fought so valiantly to return her sons to safety. Sergio and the other soldier ants lost their lives so she could be reunited with her sons, and she would never forget their valiant acts. So Queen Mariella directed her ant citizens to form a circle of life around Sergio's torn body that Bianco so bravely carried all the way back to the colony. Then she summoned everyone to pray to honor Sergio and all the other soldier ants that died so bravely and courageously. Her words of wisdom echoed throughout the colony, 'Sergio's and the other soldier ants' courageous love for our colony is the reason I still glory in the love of my sons, so we give thanks. May we all learn from their acts of bravery and love?'

Queen Mariella then turned to her sons. 'Dulio, I hope you learned how important it is to accept others as they are. We need to see their differences as gifts that make us all stronger and better. When we are united, all our differences become strengths that make us better than we are; like the different colors and threads of the ken-te clothe (a brightly colored, hand woven ceremonial clothe of the Ashanti African tribe).' Upon hearing this, Dulio was humbled and realized that his actions were selfish and inconsiderate. He now realized that bullying others to be like him were 'his bad'.

Turning to Bianco, Queen Mariella said, 'I hope you now see that you are truly amazing the way you are. . There's no need to change, for our interests and beliefs make us who we are: stronger and better. There's no need to run away from who you are. You need to stand up for what you believe and be courageous like your father, Javier.

When Bianco heard this, he was reminded of the crow's message and his father's voice ringing in his head. Right then and there he knew that there was no need to be bullied into becoming someone he wasn't. He now understood that you're not less of a living thing if you don't like fighting and have other interests instead."

"¡Abuelito, esta era un historia maravillosa!" gritÓ Ramiro.

"Yes Grandpa, that's a real good story. You're the best storyteller!" replied Diego.

"And you guys are the best, too. Estan los mejores, tambien. You're the best grandsons and now I know you'll be able to get along better."

"You're right, Grandpa. ¡Muy bien, Abuelito! Now we know why Ramiro and I should get along with each other, and I'll never try to bully him anymore.

"Fantastico, Diego. Su familia es importante and it's important to get along with one another. And that's the whole point of the story. Stand up and be courageous for who you are and learn how to appreciate the differences of others."

"Let's go have some cookies and milk!"

About the Author

Dr. James P. Menconi received his PhD. in Educational Leadership at Loyola University, Chicago. He was principal at the Monroe Elementary School in Chicago which served a Hispanic community for 15 years. He was an exchange student at the University of Guadalajara and lived in Mexico for six months. He also taught at Triton College and Malcolm X College. After retirement from his principalship he was a teacher mentor with Northwestern University's NU Teach Program. His experiences in life and in his career taught him the importance of teaching our children not to bully one another.

www.ingramcontent.com/pod-product-compliance
Lightning Source LLC
LaVergne TN
LVHW070454080526
838202LV00035B/2828